Not With A I

GWS

COLYTON GRAMMAR SCHOOL

Dewey: 822 HAR

NOT WITH A BANG

First performed at The Coliseum Theatre, Oldham, on 10th September, 1983 with the following cast of characters:

Nobby Clarke	Dennis Blanch
Tommy, Ken's dad	Bernard Latham
Paula, Nobby and Norma's daughter	Jane Hollowood
Norma	Diana Bishop
Eileen, Tommy wife and Ken's mum	Brenda Elder
Bella, Nobby's mum	Elizabeth Kelly
Ken, Paula's husband	Philip Childs

Directed by Pat Trueman
Designed by Peter Skerrett

The action takes place in the Clarkes' living-room and outside an army barracks

Time—the present

ACT I

Scene 1 The Clarkes' living room. A Sunday afternoon in winter
Scene 2 The same. Evening
Scene 3 The same. A week later. Evening
Scene 4 The same. A week later. Evening
Scene 5 The same. A few days later. Early morning
Scene 6 The same. A few days later. Evening

ACT II

Scene 1 The same. Three months later. Night
Scene 2 The same. The next day. Mid-afternoon
Scene 3 The same. Evening
Scene 4 The same. Evening
Scene 5 The same. Morning
Scene 6 Outside an army barracks. Evening
Scene 7 The Clarkes' living room. Morning

ACT I

Scene 1

The living-room of the Clarkes' house in Buttermere Avenue. A Sunday afternoon in winter

We should get the impression of a fairly well-off working-class family. A door leads off to the kitchen; another door leads to the hall and outside. There is a table set with food covered with a tablecloth and a sideboard with various bottles of drink, glasses etc. Several chairs, a settee and an armchair complete the set

As the Lights dim, the old Randolph Sutton 78 r.p.m. record of "Soldiers of the Queen" starts to play. The lighting on the stage changes to afternoon light in winter and the music fades

Nobby Clarke comes in from the hall wearing an SAS-type balaclava and carrying a Walther MPL gun. The effect should be very menacing. He sidles to the kitchen door covering himself with the gun, kicks it open, covers the interior with the gun, steps back carefully into the room

Tommy comes in from the hall, unseen by Nobby. He is carrying a lot of things for the party—cake tins, trays etc., over which he can hardly see. He drops a silver-plated tray with a loud bang

Nobby drops to the floor, then hauls himself up the settee, holding his heart

Nobby Chuffin' 'eck. (*Fighting for breath*) Chuffin' 'eck. You mad (*breath*) you dozy (*breath*) ... You frightened the ... (*breath*) doobries out of me then.

Tommy (*picking up the tray and examining it carefully*) It's Eileen's best tray this. I think I've dented it.

Nobby (*still struggling for breath*) You're dented. (*Breath*) You could kill people doing things like that you dozy ... (*breath*) ... prat.

Tommy (*putting trays etc. on the table, taking sandwiches out of cake tins etc.*) What were you doing fannyin' about like that anyway? You look like you fell off a jar of marmalade.

Nobby (*taking the balaclava off*) I was just practising what that SAS bloke showed us last week. Some Arab terrorists were holding hostages in the kitchen. I was just going to throw a stun grenade in the twin-tub and take them out when you came in.

Tommy You'll be all right in the SAS you, providing the enemy don't drop trays—then you'll crap yourself.

Nobby (*disgruntled*) I just wasn't expecting you, that's all.

Tommy (*changing the subject*) That's a funny looking gun?

Nobby Ay, it's a replica. It's a Walther MPL. West German. Standard issue for the police and border guards. It's brilliant—look. It's got a sideways folding stock, blowback loading system block and spring mechanism. Weight five kilograms. Selective fire. Rate of fire five hundred and fifty rounds per minute. Calibre nine millimetre. It's got an amazing reloadin' system.

Tommy They've got some good gear, the Germans. Better than the rubbish they give us. The women are a long time, aren't they.

Nobby Ken's gone back in the car for them. They were yapping away when I left them. They'll be there all day. "Go and get the fire lit," they said. "We won't be long." That was nearly an hour ago. It's a wonder that one of mine hasn't got frayed lips with the talking she does.

They both stand in front of the fire with their backs to it, warming their backsides and their hands

Tommy It went well, Nobby.

Nobby Not bad, it didn't take as long as I thought it would.

Tommy Sometimes that's the best thing you can say about a religious ceremony. At least it was short.

Nobby The one before us wet itself.

Tommy I never saw that.

Nobby They must have forgotten to put his plastic pants on. As soon as Father O'Connor wet his head it peed on his feet. He looked up at the roof as though it were coming in there. Then he kept lookin' at the water jug to see if it had a hole in it.

Tommy I wondered what he was doing. I saw him afterwards outside the church telling one of the altar boys to get a set of ladders and climb up on the roof and see where the water was coming in.

Nobby Do you want a quick one before the rest of them get back?

Tommy The answer to that is: Can a duck swim? and Is the Pope a Catholic? Ay.

Nobby Scotch or beer?

Tommy I'll have a Scotch.

Noises off in the hall indicate that the others have arrived back. Paula and Norma come in first with the baby, followed by Eileen, a handkerchief over her mouth, obviously forcing herself to cough

Norma Come on, love, she'll be wanting her feed soon and we'll want to keep her warm.

Paula (*laughing*) Mum, don't fuss. She'll be all right.

Norma 'Ey wasn't she a little love. She only cried the once just when the cold water took her breath away. (*Turning to Nobby*) You two got back quick.

Nobby Well I thought you wanted us to get the 'ouse warm.

Paula I don't suppose the fact that a direct line from St John's Boscos to our house passes right through the *World's End* pub and that Jonjo

Higgins would be in there with your winnings from yesterday's racing had anything to do with it at all did it?

Nobby Who me? Perish the thought. Now what's the drill. Where's these sandwiches?

Eileen and Norma have drawn the cloth off and are putting the finishing touches to the christening party. Eileen goes over to the baby

Eileen Ooh isn't she lovely, wasn't she good?

Paula D'you want to hold her, Auntie Eileen?

Eileen No, love. I'd love to but I'm frightened it will put my back out. Me back hasn't been right all this week. I bent down to pick a letter up the other day, just inside our front door and I'm sure a draught came through the letter box and caught me on the kidneys.

Nobby Now, Tommy, you get the girls a drink while I have another look at me first grandchild. (*He looks down at the baby*) Hey, she is bonny isn't she?

Tommy gets drinks for the women

Eileen Have you got any paracetamol, Norma? Me 'ead's bangin' like a Sally Army drum.

Norma I'll just get you some out of me 'andbag. (*She does so*)

Tommy (*coming over to the baby*) Ay isn't she a little love.

Paula sits down and undoes her blouse to breast-feed the baby. Both men look away, embarrassed, not knowing in which direction to look

'Em don't you want to go in the bedroom to do that, love?

Paula No, I'm all right here thanks, Uncle Tommy. Oh you were hungry, weren't you, love. There that's better, isn't it?

Nobby (*staring at the ceiling*) Where's Ken?

Paula He's gone in the car for Nanna. She said she wasn't getting in and getting squashed up with us lot, and anyway she wanted to stay behind and talk to Father O'Connor.

Tommy (*to Nobby*) She's a rare 'un your Mam, Nobby. Amazin' for her age.

Nobby They don't make 'em like that any more, Tommy. They broke the mould when they made 'er. Nine kids she brought up in a two-up and two-down.

Tommy First up best dressed.

Nobby Down the wash-house twice a week with our Mary pushin' the old pram, doin' all the washing for eleven.

Tommy Sheep's head and barley broth, dripping on toast.

Nobby Tripe and onions in milk, kitchen floor full of cockroaches every mornin'. Switch the light on they'd run all over yer bare feet.

Tommy Down the pawnshop on a Monday with the old man's suit.

Nobby Gettin' it out tea-time on a Friday so he could go out. Do you remember?

Tommy Ay, drawing boils with a hot milk bottle. Warm it up, stick it on, when it cooled it sucked all the pus out.

Nobby She used to put boot polish on me canvas pumps so they looked like shoes. Our rent man thought we were Chinese. He used to knock on the door and we used to shout "Shin tin".

Tommy Happy days, ay Nobby?

Nobby Carryin' me dad 'ome from the pub every Friday night.

Tommy Could drink, your old fella, couldn't he?

Nobby Drink! He said once he was going to have his toes amputated so he could get closer to the bar. Never missed. Always down the pub, nine o'clock every night. Price of his five Woodies and his pints, he was happy as a king. Me mam never knew how much he earnt you know. She never saw his wage packet, never.

Tommy He was a good brickie, your old man.

Nobby He was one of the best.

Bella enters, with a motor-bike helmet, wellies and a leather jacket on

Bella (*as she enters*) He was a four-eyed, bandy, drunken, shiftless old nowt and you take after him, you big fat lump.

Nobby (*taken aback*) Hello, Mother. Would you like a drink?

Bella Ay, I'll have a bottle of Guinness if you've got one. (*She removes her motor-bike gear and puts on her slippers*)

Norma Why've you come on your moped, Bella?

Bella I told Ken I wanted my own transport. I'm not having him driving me 'ome when he's had a drink. I'd rather hit me own lamppost. (*She takes a large swig from her Guinness*) Where is he any road? He left before me.

Paula He might have stopped off for ciggies or something. Have a sandwich, Nan.

Bella Ay, I will, I'm that hungry I could eat a 'orse between two bread vans.

Ken comes in

Nobby Where've you been? Me mam's been back ages.

Ken (*grinning wryly*) She's a right to be back. She went flying past me on Shaw Road and I was doing fifty.

Bella Well I can't stand hangin' about.

Tommy How do you manage to make a moped go so fast?

Bella I got the lad from across the road to zoop it up a bit.

Eileen That one that's one of those Hell's Angels?

Bella Ay, he's a smashin' lad. I sew his badges on for him and he mends my bike.

Nobby You get worse the older you get, honest you do.

Nobby takes a sandwich. He picks up a lettuce leaf and puts what he thinks is salad cream on it. People are variously seated and standing. He eats the lettuce leaf, lets out a yell and clutching his face runs into the kitchen shouting unintelligibly

Norma What's up with him?

Tommy It's the male menopause. I had it meself last week.

Nobby comes out again amost immediately with a glass of water

Nobby I've put mustard on me piggin' lettuce! Who put bloody mustard in that dish, we always have salad cream in that dish?

Norma I did. I don't want a tube of Colman's on the table. Not at a christening party, I don't. I'm sorry.

Nobby I could have died of shock. I've nearly burnt me gullet out.

Norma Well I'm sorry, but I didn't do it on purpose, you know.

Nobby Well it was a bloody stupid trick to do anyway.

Norma Look, I've said I'm sorry, 'aven't I?

Nobby So that's supposed to make it better, is it? Me mouth's red raw.

Bella Well if you leave it alone it might heal up, you never know. Anyway I always said God wasted a good arse when he put teeth in that.

Eileen I knew a man once, drank caustic soda from a lemonade bottle. Burnt his vocal cords right out, you know. He had to have a platinum tube in his neck to speak out of.

Nobby (*hoarsely*) Well you are cheerful, you are.

Eileen It fell out once in the chip shop and somebody trod on it.

Tommy (*changing the subject, talking to Paula*) How are the night-school classes going, Paula?

Paula All right. I'm really enjoying it now. I don't feel as daft as I used to. I've got the hang of it now. (*She puts the baby in the pram*)

Norma exits to the kitchen

Tommy How many nights do you go?

Paula Two nights a week and Thursday afternoons.

Tommy Who minds the baby?

Paula Ken does.

Nobby Ken?

Paula It's only for a couple of hours.

Nobby (*to Ken*) You're too soft with her, mate, that's your trouble, give 'em an inch and they'll take a mile. Next thing you know you'll be cookin' yer own tea.

Paula He does, two nights a week and Thursday afternoons.

Ken I don't mind, I like cookin', it gives me something to do. After I've been down and signed on I go in the library for a couple of hours and have a bit of a read and then I come home and start the tea. I don't mind, I like it.

Eileen I think it's terrible after all the hard work he's put in. He just comes out of his time and they sack him.

Paula There's nothing anywhere either. He's been all over again this week.

Ken I told the bloke on the desk, I says, "Look, I'm a skilled electrician and I've been out of work two and a half years, what chance have I got?" Do you know what he said? "Move south." I said "We're living in a council house, no money, no job and two hopes—Cape of Good Hope and Bob Hope. I can just see someone in Chelmsford wanting an exchange to our estate, can you?" He said "You'll just have to keep trying." I said "Have

you any idea how much bus fares and postage costs. I'm sick of walking
the streets and writing away, it's cost me a packet."

Bella Well don't blame me. I didn't vote for the bugger—but there's some
here that did. (*She looks at Nobby*)

Everyone else looks down or away

Nobby Don't bring politics up now, Mother.

Norma comes in from the kitchen with a plate of ham

Norma Here, I've cut some more ham. Help yourselves.

Nobby Did you know Ken here cooked the tea three nights a week.

Norma It just shows that not everybody's hopeless in the 'ouse. (*Pointing at
Nobby*) When I was in hospital last year I left him on his own for a week.
He rang up half-way through and asked me how the oven worked. He'd
been to the chip shop every night for his tea and he were fed up. He
fancied doin' himself a chop and some baked potatoes, he bought the
chop from Dewhursts and he couldn't work the oven for the spuds.

Nobby Well, it's the timer, I can't get it to work.

Bella You put it on that Spanish setting, son, manual, as in manual labour,
something you know bugger-all about.

Paula (*changing the subject*) Is she all right, Nanna?

Bella (*looking in the pram*) Ay, she's sleeping lovely. Ay, she's a bonny little
lass, Paula. She has your looks you know.

Nobby Well she wouldn't be much good with his. (*Pointing to Ken*)

Bella She wouldn't be much good with yours either, would she, son? Mind
you, she's got your big fat belly.

Nobby (*offended and holding himself in all of a sudden*) That's me shirt.

Bella Well they must be selling bloomin' good shirts at C and A nowadays,
you look like the humpfront of Notre Dame.

Nobby I'll soon get that off at camp.

Bella At camp! A fortnight running round Ilkley Moor with a load of other
daft nanas with pop guns shouting "bang" and stickin' labels on each
other saying' "dead". You've no chance of shiftin' that belly in a
fortnight.

Nobby It's relaxed muscle.

Bella It's a right to be relaxed, it knows there's nothin' going to happen to
it.

Things go quiet for a bit and then Eileen, apropos of nothing, says:

Eileen They're funny things, muscles. I had spasms in me muscles once. Me
leg kept twitching on its own. I couldn't stop it try as I would. That was a
muscle. The doctor said he'd never seen anything like it. When I went in
he said "Sit down here, Mrs Thompson." Well, I sat down on the chair
and he bent down to look at me and me leg jumped up and kicked him in
the stomach. He was coughing and 'owling, it was that Irish one it was
that hung himself in the airing cupboard. Anyway when he came round he
told me to sleep with me legs tied together. I only tried it one night. I got
up next morning, forgot I was tied up and fell flat on me face.

The Lights fade slightly as Bella talks to the audience

Bella (*to the audience*) So there we were. Happy families. Not much to choose between us and a lot of others. Paula there, she's me granddaughter, a grand lass. Passed her eleven plus and went to grammar school. She did well too, got her O levels and then left to get a job 'cos all her mates were working. She regrets it now of course, but you can't tell 'em. She's doing A levels now at further education place. Her husband, Ken, he's a quiet lad, doesn't say much, but he's good-hearted. Nobby, over there, he's my son. He were the baby of the family so he got spoilt. (*Breath*) It shows. Tommy, over there, he's Nobby's pal. They've been pals since they were at school together. They work on the buses. Nobby's the driver. Tommy's his guard. Him and Eileen are Ken's mum and dad. Eileen, she's a bit wet really, bit of a hypochondriac too, well, a lot of a hypochondriac. If you can get it, she's had it. She thinks she's a bit above the rest of us an' all—you know the sort I mean, fruit on the sideboard and there's nobody sick in the house. Norma, there, she's my daughter-in-law. She's a smashing lass. How she puts up with our Nobby I'll never know. Nobby and Tommy and Ken, they're all in the Territorial Army together. Every weekend they're at the barracks doing something or other and three or four times a year they're away on full pay at camp somewhere like Dartmoor or Scotland or up in the Lake District. They reckon to be on training but they always come back with a beer belly and terrible hangovers that they have to work off for a fortnight.

During the last part of Bella's speech, the men exit, Nobby taking his gun and balaclava with him

The women clear the table. As Bella talks, she kicks off her slippers and puts on her wellies and riding gear

Me? I come from Newcastle originally. I moved down here when I married Nobby's father. That was a canny few years back. Now I'm just peggin' on. When you get to my age, you either give in and sit in all day talking to the walls, or you do summat. And I'd rather do summat.

As she finishes her soliloquy, Bella, now in her riding gear again, makes an entrance for:

SCENE 2

The same. Evening

Paula, Eileen and Norma are on stage

Bella makes her entrance

Paula Hello, Nan.
Bella Hello, luv.

Paula (*to the baby in the pram*) Now then, chubby chops, give Nanna a
   smile.

Norma Are you all right, Bella?

Bella Ay, I'm fine, I've just been round the Evergreens reading to some of
   the old folks.

Eileen It does you credit, that I must say. I think you might have to read to
   me in a bit, me eyes are getting really funny. I was seeing double this
   morning. I was making Tommy's carry-out and I could see two of
   everything. In the end he went with half his stuff.

Bella I laid Mrs Wetherby out this morning, poor old soul.

Norma Mrs Wetherby that used to live on the corner? How old was she?

Bella Sixty-three.

Norma She was a really nice woman, Mrs Wetherby, one of the nicest in
   that home.

Bella She were a rum devil, you know. She died on the job.

Norma Mother!

Bella She did, I'm sure of it. There's a lot of them down the Evergreens 'as
   fellers. Mrs W had a bloke called Arnold. I met him a couple of times
   when I took her dinner round. Little bloke he were, more fat on a
   butcher's biro and she were a bit fat woman. I often used to think that
   when they were at it, it must have looked like a jockey on an elephant.

Paula Oh, I don't know where she gets it from, honest to God.

Bella (*laughing a bit*) No, listen, it's true, you could always tell when he were
   going to stop the night because he brought his own Weetabix. "Well," she
   said, "I'm only on a pension. I can't feed him as well."

Norma Well, I don't know!

Eileen How do you know they died—doing it?

Bella Well, I went to lay her out this morning and her teeth were under the
   pillow. So I picked 'em up, cleaned 'em and popped 'em in, you know.

Paula (*gagging a bit*) Ooh, Gran.

Bella Well, you 'ave to do. You can't bury 'em gummy. Any road, they
   were too small, they nearly fell down inside. I thought it's a funny do this.
   Any road I knew she had a spare set in her dressing-table. So I got them
   out and put them in. Well, I still couldn't work it all out. Any road, her
   Ellen came then, so I left her to finish off and I called in the butcher's on
   me way home and, just as I was paying for me mince, in come Arnold.
   Grinning from ear to ear, he was. I said "I'n't it terrible about Mrs W,"
   and he said, "Yes, shocking," and the tears were rolling down his cheeks
   and he had this mad grin—his teeth were sticking out like a handful of
   dominoes. I had to run out of the shop. He'd got the wrong teeth in. His
   eyes were crying and his mouth was grinning like them chimps off the tea
   advert. He must have realized she were dead, panicked and run off with
   the wrong teeth in.

They are laughing generally at this

Funny thing is he'll be at the funeral tomorrow too, I'll not be able to
keep me face straight, I'll be stood at the graveside with everyone else
crying and he'll be there looking like he's come up on the coupons.

The men come in, in their uniforms, and during the first bit of their conversation they are taking off their jackets, berets etc.

Nobby I don't know how the chuffin' 'eck we're expected to mod that FV six-o-four. How the chuff are we going to turn that into an SWD?

Tommy They give us all the crap three para have dragged over Ulster and Salalah and God knows where else.

Nobby Half of them were up for sale to Libya before Northern Ireland anyway. (*In the same breath*) Hello, love, is there any supper?

Norma I've done you some ribs and cabbage, it's warming in the oven.

Nobby Just the job.

Norma Will you have some, Tommy, there's plenty?

Tommy Well, if you're sure.

Norma I made enough for the three of you.

Norma exits to the kitchen

Bella I'll mash a pot of tea for you, Norma.

Bella goes into the kitchen too

Nobby Ribs and cabbage, that's the tackle to get down you, Tommy. It'll put lead in your pencil.

Tommy That's all right if you've got someone to write to.

Eileen He's off. Honestly, you'd think he was starved of it or something.

Tommy No. I can remember the last time dead clearly. We'd just been watching the Coronation on the telly and——

Eileen Tommy, that's enough.

Norma comes in with three plates of food on a tray

Nobby There you are, Ken. That'll put skin on your back like velvet. It'll stick to the insides of your ribs, that will.

Norma places the meal on the table

Norma, put the telly on, will you, so we can catch the news.

She does so, and as the men eat, plates on their knees, we hear the Newscaster's voice

Newscaster's voice ... to forty thousand had been expected. Extra police were brought in from the Thames Valley area but the demonstration passed off relatively peacefully. A number of women demonstrators were carried away when they laid down in front of the vehicles trying to enter the main gates. They later appeared before Reading magistrates where they were charged with causing an obstruction. Well, after the break, a man in Halifax who believes he's God, and how the factory that makes the peas for referees' whistles has been computerized.

The Newscaster's voice is followed by advertisements which gradually fade

Nobby They should have driven over them.

Norma Nobby!

Nobby Well—hairy-chinned lesbians, that's all they are.

Eileen They ought to be at home looking after their families instead of getting involved in things they know nothing about.

Paula I feel sorry for them. I mean, they're there in all that snow and sleet and cold.

Nobby Well, no-one asked them to do it. Anyway, they want to go and lie down in front of the Kremlin.

Bella comes in with a pot of tea

Bella What are you on about now, Enoch?

Nobby I'm not going to argue politics with you, Mother, I've told you that before.

Paula The peace camp women have just been on the news again, Nan.

Bella Oh ay. Well, as far as your dad's concerned anyone who isn't to the far right of Genghis Khan is a raving Commie.

Nobby Look—I'm not going to argue with you, but I'm telling you as far as those peace camp women are concerned, they don't know what they're talking about.

Bella Oh, and you do, do you?

Nobby We know what we know, don't we, Tommy?

Tommy Ay.

Bella And what's that when it's at home?

Nobby Never mind what it is, we know.

Bella What do you know?

Nobby We know what we know, that's all.

Bella You talk worse than me arse, you do.

Eileen I'm sure they do know what they're talkin' about, Bella.

Bella Hello, who rattled the bars of your cage?

Norma Eee, they always say you should never argue about two things— religion or politics, and they're right.

Nobby All I'm saying is we know what we know.

Ken (*standing*) Come on, Paula, I know what I know.

Paula (*getting up*) What's that?

Ken I'm knackered and knackered, in that order. I'll see you tomorrow everyone, good-night.

Paula Bye Mum, Dad, Tommy, Eileen, Nan.

Paula and Ken exit, pushing the baby off in the pram

Tommy Well, work in the morning. I reckon we should be off an' all, come on, Eileen.

Tommy and Eileen stand, say good-night and exit

Norma clears the plates etc. away and exits to the kitchen, leaving Bella and Nobby on their own

Bella I wish I knew what you knew.

Nobby Well, I'm not arguing, I'm going to bed. (*He stands*)

Bella (*frustrated*) I know what's the trouble with you, our Nobby.

Nobby What's that?

Bella (*slamming her helmet on*) I didn't kick your backside enough for you when you were little.

Nobby Well, it's too late now. (*Walking to the door*) Good-night, Mother.

Nobby exits to the hall

The Lights fade slightly as Bella speaks to the audience

Bella (*to the audience*) Eee, he got me so mad at times I could have killed him. He weren't bad in a lot of ways but his politics—well. He were like a lot of them, made a few bob and forgot where they come from. Convenient memories they have. (*During the next part of her speech, Bella removes her helmet and wheels on the pram and baby from the wings*) Anyway the row was all forgotten about in a couple of days and I don't suppose anything more would have happened if Paula hadn't been going to further education classes in history because the next week——

At that moment Paula walks through the hall door

—she came home and I could tell that something was up from the moment she walked through the door. The men were at the barracks weapons training or something, Norma had gone to see Eileen and I was minding the baby. (*She picks the baby up from the pram*)

SCENE 3

The same. Evening

Bella walks over to Paula with the baby in her arms

Bella Are you all right, love, you look a bit peaky.

Paula Actually, Nan, I feel as sick as a chip.

Bella Well, come on, sit down and I'll get you a cup of tea, there's one just brewed in the pot.

Paula Please, Nan.

Bella Here, go to your mam, love, she's been as good as gold while you've been out.

She hands the baby to Paula and goes out to the kitchen returning very quickly with a cup of tea

There you are. Now what's up? Is it summat you ate?

Paula No. I don't feel sick like that, Nan, it's, well, I suppose I'm depressed really. We've just had a lecture and film tonight on the Second World War and it really upset me. It was awful.

Bella You don't have to tell me, pet, we got bombed out of Royton in nineteen forty-two, you know.

Paula I've never taken much notice of it before, you know, you see bits on television but you don't take any of it in really; somehow it's just, well, it's unreal. It's almost like a story, you know. But Mr Phillips, tonight, was talking about Hiroshima and Nagasaki and he had a film from Japan. It was terrible, horrible, disgusting—two of the blokes on the course nearly fainted and they were grown men.

Norma enters

Norma Hello, are you all right, Paula? What's up, you look proper peaky? (*She takes off her hat and coat*)

Paula Ay, I'm all right, Mum, we had a film at night school about Hiroshima and it was really terrible. I mean, it brings home to you what it must have been like. I'm not kidding, it really does. There were little babies just turned into cinders. You could hardly tell what they were, school children had just melted, you could see their shadows burnt into the walls. (*She shudders*) I mean, when you've got kids of your own, it really makes you think, I mean it, that could happen to Lucy.

Norma It won't happen, don't be daft. They're all too frightened to use it.

Paula I'm not so sure, Mam, if you look at some of the lunatics we've got running the world today.

Bella Ay, they said there was going to be no war in nineteen thirty-nine. Peace in our time, they said. Peace with honour, a silly man with an umbrella and a piece of paper. Six years later we were climbing out of the ashes.

Paula What's to stop it all happening again?

Norma (*to Paula*) You've got yourself all worked up, love.

Paula It just made me feel so—I don't know—so, so powerless. You know, what I mean is, I mean I want to live, I've given life to this baby here. I want her to have a future, I want her to live; and I don't know if she will have a future the way things are going on.

Norma Look, Paula, (*more concerned*) it's no use getting morbid about it, you're going to get yourself all upset. (*She sits down and puts her arms round her*) You don't want to go worrying yourself about things like that, there's no point in worrying about things that won't happen.

Paula But who would have thought in nineteen forty-five that that was going to happen to those poor people in those cities in Japan? Nobody thought it was going to happen then, did they? But it did.

For a moment Norma can't think of anything to say. When she does it's with an air of exasperation almost

Norma Ay, well, it won't happen. It's not worth thinking about, honestly, love. You're worrying about nothing.

There is a slight pause here, then the Lights fade slightly as Bella stands and, putting her coat on, turns to face the audience. During Bella's speech, Paula exits with the baby

Bella Well, the next week Paula took us all out to see a film that was on at the night school. One of the teachers had got hold of it. He'd rented it. It was called "The War Game". It had been made for the BBC, they'd been and paid for it to be made and everything, but it had been so horrific they were frightened of showing it. They were frightened of what people would think, so they shelved it. You still can't see it on telly. There's freedom for you.

Bella exits

SCENE 4

The same. The Lights come back up. Evening

Nobby and Ken enter

Nobby Are you going out?

Norma (*putting on her coat*) Yes, we're going to see a film at our Paula's college.

Nobby You've not forgotten it's our dominoes night, have you? What about our supper?

Norma I've made your sandwiches, there's enough for all of you and they're in the kitchen like they always are. What are you worrying about?

Paula enters with the baby, fastening her blouse up as though she's just fed her

Paula Do you think you can manage to eat them on your own or do you want us to chew them up for you and all?

Nobby grunts

She should sleep right through now, Ken.

Ken I'll be all right, if she wakes up I'll just change her and play with her for a bit. She'll soon go back down.

Paula (*putting the baby in the pram*) Don't go waking her up just so you can play with her, I know what you do when me back's turned. You'll have her spoilt.

Ken I won't.

There is a knock, off

Norma (*putting her hat on*) Come in.

Tommy and Eileen come in. Tommy is carrying a crate of beer. Eileen is blowing her nose

Eileen I'll not come near the baby. I've got this terrible head-cold that's gone to me chest. I knew I was going to get it when I stood near that man at the bus stop whooping and coughing and splutterin' he was all over the place. I bet the whole bus queue's laid up by now, some people have got no consideration.

Paula What did the doctor say yesterday when you went to see him about your back?

Eileen Ooh, I was weary when I came out. He gave me so many examinations. He said he'd never seen a pair of lungs on a woman my age like it. He said "They're marvellous your lungs." The trouble is he thinks it's me feet now.

Bella Your feet? Well I'll go to the foot of our stairs. How can your feet give you pains in the back?

Eileen He says "All your troubles, Mrs Thompson, could be trapped nerves in your feet. It's very uncommon but I do believe we could have an uncommon case here." He looked at me womb as well.

Tommy Leave it out will you Eileen.

Eileen (*giving him a sideways glance*) Well I'll tell you all about it in the car.

The women exit

Nobby goes into the kitchen with the beer

Tommy takes a box of dominoes from the sideboard, shakes them out on to the table and begins shuffling them

Tommy (*shouting*) Nobby.

Nobby comes in with three glasses of beer

Come on you'll have it dark. (*To Ken*) Come on Ken, shuffle them.

Ken starts shuffling them vigorously

Nobby All right, don't rub the bloody spots off 'em.

Tommy Come on Nobby, you to pick up.

Nobby I'll never understand women, you won't believe what she's done. (*He leads the dominoes*)

Ken Fancy starting off with that!

Tommy What's she done? (*He puts down a domino*)

Nobby (*indicating the kitchen*) Well she's made the sandwiches like she usually does but she's forgotten to put piccalilli on 'em.

Tommy (*genuinely shocked*) But she always puts piccalilli on the 'am sandwiches. She knows we like piccalilli when we're playing dominoes. We never have 'am sandwiches without piccalilli on 'em. 'Am without piccalilli is like Laurel without Hardy. Like Jekyll without Hyde—like the two Ronnies without one of them.

Ken (*playing a domino*) Well why can't you put some on yourself?

Nobby I don't know where she keeps it.

Ken (*amazed at Nobby's stupidity*) Well, bugger me.

Nobby (*playing*) Go on try that for size.

Tommy Have you seen that new bird in traffic? Beautiful legs she has, all the way up to her bum. Huge knockers. Gi'enormous. Whopping.

Nobby Did you play that five-one then Ken?

Ken Yeah, you played the three-one and I put the five-one down.

Tommy (*carrying on regardless, in a world of his own*) She had no bra on today and she ran down them iron steps in the depot, you know the ones near the canteen, and some of the lads saw her coming down the steps. Chalky White dropped a spanner in a diesel tank and Big Robbo ran a number four into the back of a number seventeen.

Nobby (*ignoring him*) Well, who the bloody hell put that five-four across as a double-five?

Ken Me dad did.

Nobby (*to Tommy*) Here, bloody concentrate you, you've buggered the bloody game up.

Tommy Oh ay, so I have, I thought it were a double-five.

Ken I'll get the sandwiches.

Ken exits to the kitchen

Nobby See if you can find where she keeps the piccalilli. (*To Tommy*) Here, shuffle them.

Ken (*off*) It's here right in front of the cupboard.

Nobby Which cupboard?

Ken (*off*) The one over the fridge.

Nobby I didn't know we had a cupboard there.

Ken comes in with the sandwiches and piccalilli and the baby starts making snuffling noises as he puts them on the table

Ken Ay up, she's snuffling a bit.

Nobby She's not hungry is she? (*He gets up and looks in the pram*)

Ken Well if she is there's not much I can do about it. If I feed her the 'airs on me chest'll make her sneeze. No she shouldn't be hungry, Paula just fed her before she went out. She's probably got a dirty nappy.

Nobby Oh. (*He goes back to the table and starts spooning the piccalilli on to the ham sandwiches*)

Ken lifts the baby out and starts to change her nappy on the settee. This scene can be funny but it mustn't go over the top and become totally crude

Tommy You know that's something I never did.

Nobby Me neither, I wouldn't know where to begin.

Ken It's dead easy when you've done it once.

Tommy (*pointing to Ken*) He were lay on the hearthrug once when he was a baby when Eileen were changin' 'im. Stark naked he was. He piddled and it went straight up in the air and landed in his eye. He didn't half yell. (*He laughs*)

Nobby (*still ladling out the piccalilli*) That's the problem with your nudger. It starts getting you into trouble from the minute you're born. (*He sits down and starts eating a sandwich*) By, that's better. They're not the same without piccalilli aren't 'am sandwiches.

Ken (*to the baby*) Who's done a pooey nappy then? Who's done a great big stinky pooey nappy?

Tommy has picked up a sandwich too and is shuffling the dominoes

Who's done a great big dump in her nappy? (*To Nobby and Tommy*) It's funny you know, but with her still being on her mother's milk it's always bright yellow. (*He shows them*)

Nobby (*looking at his sandwich*) Turn it in will you.

Tommy Oor, leave it out Ken. (*He looks disgustedly at his sandwich*)

Ken What's up?

Tommy I think I could 'ave done without that piccalilli Nobby.

Nobby I don't know what you want messing about with 'er nappies for anyway. Our Paula could have done that when she got back.

Ken (*to the baby*) There you are my little duchess, now go on fast back to beddy byes. (*He puts her back in the pram*)

Tommy Come on we want another game, you'll have it dark.

Ken (*sitting down*) Right, fives and threes again. Let's get you knocking. Pound in first out collects.

They all put a pound down on the table and they play for a bit

Nobby Fives and twos never loses.

Ken I'll take off that five so me dad's stuck with his double.

Tommy You can bugger off.

Nobby Old country closet, double-one.

Ken Now you've buggered it, I'll have to threes it up.

Nobby You dozy bugger, you've stopped the game. (*To Tommy*) Are you knocking?

Tommy (*knocking*) Ay.

Nobby (*knocking*) I'm knocking too.

Ken Three six (*putting a domino down*) and you're both still knocking, double-six and three is fifteen. (*Playing his double-six*) That's eight, that's me pegged out and thank you very much for a couple of quid.

Nobby Well bugger me, I've seen some playing in my life. There was no use me trying to do anything then, I had a hand like a foot. (*He puts the dominoes away*)

The women come in, very quiet and obviously thoughtful

(*To Norma*) Are you all right, love? Was it a good film was it? What was it? A romance?

There is no answer

You know what you forgot don't you? You forgot the piccalilli.

Norma You can stuff the piccalilli!

Tommy (*exchanging glances with Nobby, to Eileen*) Em, did you enjoy the film love?

Eileen ignores him. The men look at each other and shrug

Paula I'll put the kettle on Mum.

Paula exits to the kitchen

Norma I still can't believe I've seen what I've seen. It's disgustin'.

Nobby What?

Norma (*almost exasperated at having to explain something that affected her so deeply emotionally*) This—film we've just seen, it, it was . . . it was just incredible. It's the most terrifying thing I've ever seen.

Nobby You shouldn't go and see those horror films if they upset you like that.

Norma (*shouting at him*) It weren't a horror film you daft pillock. It were a documentary.

Ken (*sensing trouble*) I'll just go and help Paula with the tea then.

Ken exits to the kitchen

Nobby (*putting both feet right in it now*) What 'ave you got yourself upset over a bloody film for?

Norma (*almost unbelievingly*) You stupid, brainless . . . (*She pauses as she is lost for words*) . . . pillock.

Nobby (*shocked and at the same time a little menacing*) You what?

Tommy (*half-standing*) Come on Eileen, we'd better go home.

Eileen Just sit down.

Tommy does as he's told

Norma (*to Nobby*) We've just seen a film tonight that shows what would happen if a nuclear bomb fell on a town like this.

Nobby Oh. And?

Norma (*amazed rather than angry*) And? And? You should have seen it that's all. Those that were blown up were the lucky ones. The rest of them were walking round with burns, radiation sickness, there was a fireball sucking people into the centre from miles away, the hospitals were destroyed, nearly all the doctors were killed, nearly all the nurses. What few doctors there were, were trying to treat people and the police were shooting people the doctors couldn't save.

Paula and Ken come in from the kitchen with a tray of tea

Paula There were curfews, the army shooting into crowds of people.

Tommy You don't want to go watchin' things like that.

Bella What do you want us to watch, *Emmerdale Farm*? *Crossroads*? *Jackanory*?

Eileen I never realized before tonight what it would be like. They're mad to even think of using them, these politicians.

Nobby What do you mean?

Norma Bombs and missiles, that's what she means.

Tommy We 'ave to 'ave 'em.

Eileen Why?

Nobby The Russians have got 'em.

Norma Suppose the Russians did bomb us. Do you think that would justify us killing the ordinary men, women and children in Russia?

Nobby Course it would.

Tommy Yes, if they bombed us. It's revenge.

Norma So, if some mad swine in Russia pressed the button and flattened us, we could kill them?

Tommy Course.

Paula You're puddled, both of you.

Nobby But it won't happen.

Bella Why not?

Nobby Because we're both too frightened to use them.

Bella Then why 'ave them then?

Nobby What? You what?

Bella If you're not going to use them then why have them?

Tommy So that they can't use theirs, it's, em, it's a deterrent in't it.

Bella So we have them not to use so that they won't use theirs and they have theirs not to use so that we won't use ours.

Nobby Em, er, yes in a way.

Paula So we have them not to use to fight a war that if we do fight we lose?

Nobby Well, em, er.

Norma You're bloody puddled you are.

Nobby (*exasperated*) They're threats that's all. We have to 'ave 'em. They threaten us and we threaten them.

Paula exits to the kitchen

Norma Well just suppose we didn't threaten them?

Nobby What do you mean? If we didn't threaten them they'd still threaten us.

Norma How do you know: have you ever tried it? How do you know that the Russians don't want peace as much as we do. They probably do in fact.

Nobby You're barmy. The trouble is you shouldn't get involved in this. It's too complicated for women.

Paula comes in with the milk-jug in her hands

Paula You what? (*She raises the milk-jug over his head*) Too complicated for what? (*She is getting really mad and is about to pour it over his head*)

Norma (*calmly*) Don't do that love. That's what he'd expect. But we won't win with violence that's their way. There has to be another way. (*She turns away slightly then puts her mouth close to his ear and roars*) You brainless pillock!!!!

Nobby spills his tea over his leg

(*To Paula*) You see?

Nobby jumps up and runs to the kitchen to wipe himself down. Tommy goes with him. Ken sidles out

There is a slight fade as Bella steps forward to talk to the audience. During her speech, Paula exits with the baby and pram, Eileen and Norma exit with teacups etc.

Bella Well, funny enough the next night in the *Chron* there were a letter from a woman about the very thing we'd been talking about. (*She takes a piece of newspaper in her hand and reads out loud*) "I am an ordinary working class housewife and mum. I don't know very much about politics, but I do know that the more I have read about nuclear weapons in the papers, the more afraid I get. I don't think I could join an organization like CND because I don't know enough about it. But can't ordinary women like myself get together and do something about it, even if only talk? I've hired a room with my own money in the *Sun Inn* in Sandgate for this Thursday evening, from seven o'clock onwards. Any women who are interested in coming along to talk about nuclear weapons and peace, are welcome." (*She stops reading*) So we went along. Me, Paula, Norma, and Eileen. The woman who'd written the letter was an ordinary lass, just like us. No education to speak of, no politics, just frustrated and determined not to take it all without fighting. She'd expected three or four—nearly a hundred turned up and we decided to form the Deepdale Women's Peace Movement. We didn't know anything about organization and we didn't really want to know anything about organization, there was no chairman, there was no committee, we were just all involved in it together. One of the women knew that the next week there was going to be a big protest outside the American air base at Burtonwood, so we all decided to go along to give our support. We hired a coach. And that morning we all got up right early to catch the coach from outside the Town Hall. Of course the men didn't know anything about it.

SCENE 5

The same. Very early morning

Paula comes running in, with the baby in a sling

This scene is conducted in loud whispers

Paula Mother, are you coming or not?

Norma sticks her head round the kitchen door, with a knife in one hand and a lunchbox in the other

Norma I've just got his sandwiches to put up.
Bella Lerrim get his own, the big fat lump. Come on, we'll be late.
Norma But I always put his carry out up.
Bella Ay, I spoilt him to start with and you've carried on. Well, have a day off for a change. (*Taking the knife out of her hand*) Come on or we'll miss the bus.
Norma Ay, you're right, we'll have to hurry. I'll just leave him a note. (*She scribbles a note*)
Bella Tell him nowt, or tell him you've run off with the milkman.
Norma Our milkman! Have you seen him? He's got a face like a bucket of spam. (*She is still writing*)
Bella Come on, you'll 'ave it dark. (*Looking over Norma's shoulder*) Eh, that's good. Eh he won't like that—(*Pause*)—or that! He'll be blazing. (*Pause*) That'll cap him.
Norma Right. I'll leave it there, where he'll see it.

Bella, Norma and Paula exit

The Lights increase slightly to early morning. The doorbell rings

Nobby comes down carrying his jacket, having obviously just got dressed, and lets Tommy in

Nobby All right, Tommy?

Tommy Ay, I saw the Red Baron going past on his motor-bike on the way here.

Nobby Ay, he'll be on the fifty-nines again pushin' us all the way to Shaw like a good union man. (*Noticing the mess on the table*) Here where's me carry out?

Tommy Maybe she's put it in yer box?

Nobby No, she always leaves it on the table. (*Looking round and in his box*) She hasn't made it. Bloody charmin'!

Tommy You'll have to put up for yourself.

Nobby (*pulling on his jacket*) Sod that, I'll buy some from the butty bar.

Tommy I wonder where they've all gone.

Nobby Who?

Tommy Well Eileen went out early this morning and when I asked her where she was going, she just said they were going out on a bus trip.

Nobby Have you got a carry out?

Tommy Ay, cold 'am and pickles.

Nobby So she put yours up then?

Tommy Ay, she always does.

Nobby (*seeing the note*) Hang about. She's written something down here. It will be some excuse or other. (*He reads*) "Dear Warmonger, Have gone out for the day. Your survival rations, weekend warriors for the use of, are in the fridge a, breadbin b, butter-dish c, and pickle-jar d. Put contents of c on b then add contents of a. Add bits from d, wrap in clingfilm and eat. And I hope it chokes you." (*Putting the paper down*) Bloody chuffin' 'eck—come on, we'll be late.

Nobby and Tommy exit

The Lights change. It is now evening

Nobby and Tommy enter

Nobby Well, where the 'ell can they be?

Tommy I don't know. They left about six this morning and it's seven o'clock now. It will be one of those 'en-party dos to Morecambe or Llandudno or something like that.

Nobby Well she never told me bugger all about it.

Tommy Ken said he doesn't know where Paula's gone either, but she took the baby with her.

Nobby Well are we going to have summat to eat or what?

Tommy Well what've you got in?

Nobby I'll go and have a look in the fridge.

He exits to the kitchen

(*Off*) Bloody marvellous. She's not been shopping again. I think she's trying to kill me slowly by starvation. When she does cook anyway it's a disaster. Do you know what she did last week?

Tommy What?

Nobby (*sticking his head round the door*) Cooked a chicken with the giblets in.

Tommy What's wrong with that?
Nobby (*going back in*) In a bloody polythene bag?
Tommy Oh.

Nobby reappears with some stuff on a plate

Nobby Here you are, that's all there is.
Tommy What is it?
Nobby Chicken leg, a bit of cheese, some raspberry jelly and half a stick of celery.
Tommy Bloody 'ell! I think we should go to the carry out.
Nobby It doesn't open till nine o'clock. (*He turns on the TV*)

They sit down. The Newscaster's voice fades up

Newscaster's Voice ... tonwood earlier this afternoon. There were a number of arrests made and two policemen were slightly injured in scuffles with demonstrators. Rain kept the numbers down, but it's still estimated that more than ten thousand people were present.
Nobby (*dropping his chicken leg*) It's me mam! Chuffin' 'eck! It's me mam! There's two policemen pickin' her up.
Tommy There's Eileen and Norma and Paula! Bloody 'ell fire.

The sound of the Greenham Common song is heard

Nobby Look at that, me mam's gone back and lay down again. And Norma and Eileen, chuffin' 'eck, I'll kill 'em.
Newscaster's Voice And now news of the Widnes search.

Nobby turns off the TV

Tommy Well, chuff me, I can't believe it, it's incredible.
Nobby We've been too bloody soft with them, Tommy, that's the trouble, given them too much leeway. What the 'ell do they want to go and get themselves mixed up in all this women's lib crap and all that? I don't understand it!
Tommy I can't believe it. I mean they don't tell you anything. I had no idea that all this was going on. They could have got themselves arrested.

At that moment Ken bursts in

Ken Did you see it on the telly then, me mam?
Nobby (*nodding*) Ay, I'll bloody kill 'em when they get home. (*He's obviously frustrated and angry and doesn't really know what he's going to do*) What are we going to do about it? I'll bloody well murder 'er. What does she think she's playing at? You tell me?
Tommy Don't ask me. My one's in this an' all you know. I'm stoppin' 'er money. I'm not giving her 'ousekeeping to get involved in civil disorder.
Nobby It's the deceit and the lies I can't stand. No wonder there's no food in the fridge. She'd have given all the money to them Commies.
Ken Do you think they really believe it Nobby?
Nobby They've been brainwashed, like the Moonies.
Tommy That Irish family from Court Street?

Nobby No. That religion. That Moonies cult. They've been brainwashed. Typical women. No bloody commonsense. What are we going to do about it?

Ken I'm buggered if I know.

The hall door opens and the women come in. Paula has the baby

Bella I should have kicked that young bobby in the you know where. "What are you doin' out at this time Mother you should be safe at home, wrapped up and warm." I said, "Ay, when you were born they threw the best bit away."

Norma (*seeing the men*) Oh hello love, I'm sorry we're late back.

Nobby What're you doing here? We just saw you on the telly.

Norma Oh, it was on was it?

Bella (*aggressively*) Have you never heard of film then? It means they can show a picture of you in one place while you're in another. It's been about quite a while you know.

Nobby Never mind all this clever bit, what's all this about?

Norma What?

Nobby This—this peace movement crap.

Norma is a bit taken aback at first, then answers him back quietly and firmly

Norma What I do, what my beliefs are, has got nothing to do with you, Nobby, and what's more they're not crap.

Eileen She's a right to her own opinions you know Nobby.

Nobby Shut it you, you moaning minny. I happen to think they are crap.

Norma Well I don't, I happen to believe in it.

Nobby Well you can just bloody well unbelieve in it.

Norma And you can get stuffed!

There is a stunned silence here which should be held for as long as it will stand because this is the first time that Norma has really stood up to Nobby openly. Everybody is shocked. The silence is broken by Ken

Ken Er, would anybody like a cup of tea?

Paula (*shaking her head, half exasperated, half loving him*) Oh Ken, you and your flaming tea.

Ken shrugs and goes off to the kitchen

The women sit down

Nobby and Tommy exit

SCENE 6

The Lights fade as Bella steps forward to talk to the audience. As she speaks, the other women clear the table and gather the materials to make the banner. Paula wheels on the pram and puts the baby in it

Bella Well a couple of nights later, we decided we were going to go down to

Greenham Common. There was a rally on in support of the women at the peace camp. So any road, we stopped in the night before to make ourselves a banner that we could carry with us. The fellers were out at the TA so we had the house to ourselves.

The Lights come up again—evening. Bella steps back into the action

Pass me those pins, Paula.

Norma We'll have to think of a slogan.

Paula Em, "Mothers Against the Bomb"?

Norma No, we want something wilder than that.

Bella "Wild Mothers Against the Bomb."

Norma What about "Grannies Against the Bomb"?

Paula We're not all grannies though are we?

There is a pause

Eileen (*shouting*) "Bollocks to the Bomb."

They all look at her, surprised, and there is a brief pause

Bella (*picking up a brush*) How do you spell it?

Norma Bella, give up will you.

Eileen (*standing rubbing her back*) Ooh I think I've put me back out with all that bending down.

Bella Here, give me that tape. You're as much use as a chocolate tea-pot.

Noises off indicate that the men are coming back

Norma They're back early tonight.

Bella They probably ran out of caps for their guns.

Nobby (*off*) They'll be here all right. It'll be like a bloody Trotskyite cell.

Nobby, Tommy and Ken enter in uniform

Here they are, the Mata Haris of Deepdale.

Norma You're home early.

Nobby We're home early because we didn't go to the Mess for a pint afterwards and the reason we didn't go in the Mess for a pint afterwards is that we are the laughing stock of the battalion.

Paula Stocks.

Nobby (*stopped in mid-flow*) You what?

Paula Stocks—there are three of you so you have to use the plural.

Nobby (*exasperated*) Ken, Ken will you bloody well speak to 'er.

Ken Hello Paula.

Paula Hello Ken.

Nobby I don't know what's going on in this house you're all as daft as Dick's hatband.

Norma Are you going to tell us or what?

Nobby What?

Tommy I think she means what happened tonight.

Nobby Well, we got to the barracks and all three of us were sent for by Major Simpson.

Ken I've never seen him so mad.

Nobby "Clarke", he said, "if your wives do have to be involved in activities against the interests of their own country, perhaps you could convince them that Russia would be a better place for them to demonstrate their feelings or at least you could tell them to keep their pictures and their half-baked philosophies off my television screen."

Norma Well you can go right back there and tell Major Wilfred Simpson to stick to running his pork butcher's shop and keep his long piggy nose out of my bloody business.

There is a silence

Nobby I don't know what to say. I think you've gone barmy the lot of you. (*There is a pause while Nobby picks up the courage to speak*) Look, being serious now, we've been talking haven't we lads and this thing's got to stop.

Norma What has?

Nobby All this CND business.

Norma Well we'd like you to stop all this army business wouldn't we?

There is general agreement from the women

Tommy You must be joking.

Paula Why? Why must we be joking? What we're trying to do is bring about peace. What you're doing is just the opposite.

Nobby Don't talk crap.

Norma Upstairs in that wardrobe there's a nuclear and chemical suit you got last year at Preston Barracks, am I right?

Nobby So what?

Bella So that when the time comes you can keep us all in order, can't you?

Paula Blocking off all the motorways, imposing a curfew.

Norma Shooting anybody who doesn't agree with the Government and doesn't want to go to war.

Nobby (*genuinely taken aback*) Where did you get all this from?

Bella We're in the peace movement not the daft movement. We have ways of finding things out too you know, things the Government don't want us to find out.

Nobby You haven't any idea what it's all about.

Paula Of course we have. Women have always had more of an idea than men. But just because our idea of the world doesn't fit in with yours you deny it. I'll tell you what, in our world you could live, it wouldn't be perfect but at least it would try to be a fair world and a peaceful one. I've been thinking a lot recently.

Nobby It doesn't sound like it.

Paula That's all your argument isn't it, trying to make people look stupid. You think because it's always been this way that we can't ever change it. What has your world ever produced: the trenches, eight million dead in four years, Hitler (*by now she is winding herself up and getting very angry*), Belsen, Auschwitz, Babiyar, twenty-five million dead Russians, Vietnam,

My-Lai, the Lebanon. What has your world of guns and bluffs ever produced except widows and orphans?

Nobby Rubbish.

Norma It's not rubbish, it's the truth.

Bella I've seen them son, lads like you. When I was a lass I saw them coming back from the First World War the same lads that were full of the drums four years before marching off to fight the Kaiser. It'll be over by Christmas they said. Four years later they came hobbling back, the crippled, the blind, the insane, the shell-shocked ones with their minds burnt out like empty sockets, and what for? A hundred yards of mud and a politician's bloody promise. It's not us that's barmy, it's you.

Nobby You've all been brainwashed by the bloody Russians. It's the Russians that have put all the money up for this ban the bomb rubbish.

Paula You talk rubbish. The Russians have got nothing to do with it.

Nobby Well it's a Communist organization anyway.

Norma Are you calling me a Communist? I actually resent that remark. We're all Communists are we? Me, your mother, Paula, Eileen? Eileen over there she knows as much about Communism as Cyril Smith does about hang-gliding.

Paula Anyway, have you ever met any Russians?

Nobby No, and I bloody well don't want to.

Bella They were our allies in the war. Do you not remember that? Twenty-five million dead they had. They don't want another war. It's the arms manufacturers and high-ranking military and the politicians in this world that are benefiting from this arms race and nobody else. All that money that's spent on bombs and missiles, you could build thousands of hospitals. You could wipe out poverty overnight.

Nobby Bollocks!

Paula Oh, so that's the standard of your argument is it? What country is the only country in the world that has dropped the atomic bomb on people, used napalm and chemical warfare, and that supports all the rotten military dictatorships in the world? America, that's what.

There is a pause

Ken Would anyone like a cup of tea?

Paula Oh Ken, you and your bloody tea.

The baby starts crying

Bella Now look what you've done with your bloody shouting you gormless pillock.

Nobby Come on lads, we'll go to the pub. At least they talk some bloody sense there. I'm not staying here listening to this load of crap.

The men exit to the hall

Bella (*as they go*) Talk sense? You must be joking. All they talk about there are football and horses, and the women on page three of *The Sun*.

Nobby (*off*) Bollocks!

The women sit down. Paula goes towards the kitchen

Paula I'll brew up.

Paula exits

Norma It's enough to make you want to spit. Bloody men! They can't see further than their noses.

Bella (*on her knees at the banner*) There must be some way you could change their bloody minds.

Eileen (*picking up a magazine*) Well you can't expect everybody to agree with your way of thinking can you.

Norma (*exasperated*) It's their way of thinking that's going to kill us all.

Eileen Oh there's something in here about migraine and stress.

Bella My God. The world could be falling down round your ears and you'd still be trying to find summat up with you.

Eileen (*looking over the top of her paper*) No I wouldn't. (*Looking back*) Ooh look this is good. (*Reading aloud*) "Sexual warfare, the battleground of the bedroom." "Do you use sex as a weapon?" it says here.

Bella Chance would be a fine thing. It's a long time since I did anybody any damage.

Eileen "Many of the women that we interviewed admitted that they used sex or the refusal to have sex with their partners in order to get their own way, or as a punishment for a partner's misbehaviour."

Paula comes in with the tea

Paula It's ready.

Norma We could do that.

Eileen What?

Norma Go on sexual strike.

Eileen You must be jokin'.

Paula We could try it. What have we got to lose?

Eileen I don't know if me nerves would stand it. The rows and everything.

Norma I thought you'd stopped anyway?

Eileen Well, not stopped, just cut down. I mean he may not be a Casanova but he's like Beechams, dead regular, well regular and pretty dead.

Paula I think it could work you know.

Eileen But what good would it do? It would only affect us four round here.

Paula Yes, but if it worked with our men; if we got our men to give up the army by going on sexual strike then it could spread all over the world, just imagine it. All the women in the world joining together in a world-wide movement. Anyway, it's worth a try. It's the only way to hit at them— through their willies.

Norma Ay, "Women against Willies".

Paula They're so proud of them aren't they? They walk around sticking them out like they've something special. I think they're funny you know. They're either sticking up pointing at the ceiling or hanging down like a dead turkey's neck.

Norma It's Christmas all year round in our house.

Eileen You don't think it'd work do you, going on strike like that?

Paula We can try. At least we'd be doing something.

Norma She's right you know. If you think about it. It sounds stupid but then again so do a lot of other good ideas. We can't resort to violence, it's our only weapon. Are we to give it a try or what?

Paula Well I'm willing.

Eileen Well I suppose anything's worth a try.

Bella Well I'll give you moral support. Me going on sexual strike is like the eskimos demonstrating against snow. Bugger all use.

Norma (*standing*) Right, united we stand.

Paula Legs together.

Eileen Nighties tied round our ankles.

While they've been doing this Bella has been painting on the banner. She stands up with the banner and they unfurl it. It reads "No Nooky Against the Nukes". As the women stand giving the clenched fist salute——

the CURTAIN *falls*

ACT II

SCENE 1

The same. It is night-time, three months later

As the CURTAIN *rises Norma walks on stage. She is wearing a duffle coat, overalls, slippers, gardening gloves and a beret. She is tidying up generally around the room*

We hear the men off talking. They enter in uniform

Ken Hello Norma. (*Looking at his watch*) Are you going out?
Norma No I'm going to bed.
Ken Oh.
Norma If you want any supper you can make it yourselves. There's some cheese and a bit of bread and butter pudding and some ham. I haven't had time to shop today, I've been too busy. Good-night Tommy, good-night Ken.

They say good-night variously

Norma exits

Nobby (*sitting down on the settee*) Too busy. She's been at one of her chuffin' meetings with all the other nutters. I had to make my own tea tonight too.

Ken goes into the kitchen

Tommy You didn't did you?
Nobby Ay.
Tommy What did you make?
Nobby There were a tin of peas, some corned beef and a rice pudding.
Tommy Was it all right?
Nobby No, I burnt the peas, cut me bloody finger getting the corned beef out of the tin and dropped the rice pudding on the floor. I had to give it to the cat.

Ken comes back out of the kitchen

Ken You haven't got a cat!
Nobby Well, there were one there.
Ken In the kitchen?
Nobby Yes, in the bloody kitchen.

Ken goes back to look

I've lost half a stone since all this lot started.

Ken comes in laughing

Ken You'd better get your eyes seen to Nobby, you've given your tea to one of Bella's old hats.

He shows them a furry hat and goes out again

Nobby Well what it doing on the chuffin' floor any road? (*Pause*) It's driving me barmy all this, I'm starting seeing things.

Tommy It's a pity they don't still put bromide in your tea isn't it.

Ken enters with three mugs of tea

Ken I don't think I can take it much longer, Nobby, you know what I mean? I mean we've only been married a year and a bit, it's not like you pair getting old and past it.

Nobby Cheeky bugger.

Tommy It doesn't fall off when you get to forty you know—doesn't get much of an airing, but it doesn't fall off.

Ken I mean we haven't got separate beds or anything you know. I still fancy her like mad. I mean last night she came to bed with two pairs of pyjamas and a housecoat on, she turned over and we were lying there just touching like spoons in a drawer and all the blood in me body went surging down into me nudger. (*Pause*) I lay on me back for two and a half hours like a chuffin' submarine.

Tommy That happened to me an' all a couple of nights back.

Ken Did it?

Tommy Ay, only it was down periscope after twenty minutes.

Nobby (*almost distractedly, thinking out loud*) You see, you know what it is, it's lust.

Tommy You haven't just discovered this fact Nobby have you?

Nobby No, seriously, if we could subdue the fires of lust we could stand a chance of winning.

Ken It's all right for you to talk about subduing the fires of lust Nobby. I can't do it. I saw a pair of her tights hanging on the line the other day and it turned me on! And you know how stupid tights look hanging on a line!

Tommy and Nobby nod for a moment obviously deeply moved by what he's just said

Nobby But we'll just have to prove that we're stronger than them. That we're not slaves to that throbbing little dictator, that Hitler hiding in your Y-fronts.

Tommy That's very poetic that Nobby. You should take up writing you should.

Nobby I'll tell you what it is. It's true—women will use lust all the time to get their own way. It's the oldest game in the book. Eve with the old apple in the garden, Adam gives in and what happens? The landlord evicts them. Women have got three of the most terrible weapons known to man.

Ken Three?

Nobby Ay, lust, lust and—(*getting worked up*)—lust.

Pause as they all stare into space thoughtfully

Tommy (*almost as if he's dreaming out loud*) I had a right funny dream last night, I did. I dreamt I was in bed with that red-'ead in the canteen.

Nobby What's funny about that?

Tommy I dreamt we'd been to the pictures to see *The Blue Lagoon*, dead romantic it was, and then I'd taken her for a pizza on the way home. Bottle of Frascati, flaming Sambuca, the full monty. And all the time in the pictures and the pizza house she'd been touching me up you know.

Nobby Which hand?

Tommy You what?

Nobby Which hand was she touching you up with?

Tommy I can't remember! Anyway it's not important.

Nobby I'm just trying to get the full picture that's all.

Tommy Anyway the next thing is, we're back at this big house and it's in the middle of a forest like, like one of them chateaux and there's a dog in uniform with one eye opening the door.

Nobby Are you making this up?

Tommy Straight up Nobby, no bull. Anyway the next thing is we were in bed and her hands were all over me so I rolled her over and—it's bloody stupid, I can't tell you.

Nobby Go on.

Ken Come on you've started now, finish it.

Tommy No I can't tell you, it's rubbish.

Nobby Go on.

Tommy I can't.

Nobby (*grabbing him by the lapels*) If you don't tell me I'll bloody well brain you. (*He lets him go*)

Tommy Well I was just going to do the business, you know, when, ah it's stupid.

Nobby For God's sake get on with it.

Tommy Well I was just going to introduce old Fagin when she, she—she turned ...

Ken What? She turned what?

Tommy Erm, into a side of bacon.

Nobby Chuffin' 'eck you dozy prat. A side of bacon!

Tommy It was only a dream you know.

Nobby I know it was only a dream, you pillock. It can't have been real can it? One-eyed dogs in uniform and sides of bacon.

Ken You dreamt that lovely red-'ead with the freckly back from the canteen went to bed with you and turned into a side of bacon?

Tommy Yes.

Nobby You're not startin' to fancy pigs are you?

Tommy Am I 'ell as like.

Ken I think your brains are goin' Dad.

Nobby Well I've had enough, I'm kicking 'er out.

Tommy I'm getting that way meself. Three months it's been now, it's a bit much.

Ken You can't do that, where will they go?

Nobby I don't give a bugger, she can go down the Sally Army for all I care.

Tommy Well Eileen will be all right, she can probably book herself in hospital for some tests or somethin'.

Nobby What's up with 'er now?

Tommy Nothin'. But she's been on waitin' list for so many things for so long she can probably pick and choose from a couple of dozen to go on with. She's got a total choice from liver tests at Boundary Park to barium enemas at the Northern, thyroid at Salford Royal and brain scans at Christies. She's booked on 'em all for some time or another. The only thing they're not lookin' for with 'er is trouble with 'er knackers.

Ken (*who's been thinking about all this and looks worried*) Well I couldn't kick Paula out.

Nobby Why not?

Ken Well, there's the baby and there's all the payments on the furniture and stuff and anyway (*close to tears*), I love 'er.

There is a pause

Nobby (*slightly embarrassed*) Ay, well you'll get over that eventually.

Tommy We'll have to do summat. It's camp next week and we've got no clean uniforms.

Nobby We'll just have to take all our kit to the Co-op laundry. Well at least we'll have clean clothes on for a fortnight. I'm sick of trying to wash 'em. That bloody machine. I'll swear to God it swallows socks. It must 'ave eaten one of every pair of socks that I've got. I'm sure the manufacturers do something to make washin'-machines eat socks. (*Beat*) But they only eat one of the buggers. I've got at least fifteen single socks now, all different colours.

Tommy You ought to start lookin' for a one-legged rugby team.

Nobby I wish you'd bugger off with your bright ideas. Anyway I'm for bed.

Tommy Ay, we'd better be off too.

Nobby (*picking up the mugs*) Right, I'll see you in the morning, Tommy. See you Ken.

Ken Ta-rah, Nobby, see yer.

Tommy See you Nobby.

Ken and Tommy exit

Nobby goes off through the kitchen, taking the mugs with him

SCENE 2

The same. The Lights change to mid-afternoon

Paula and Bella come in from shopping, carrying bags and pushing the pram. They start unpacking the food

Bella Eee, she'll be sitting up in a bit will that one. She's bright as a button. Just look at her looking round now.

Paula She keeps trying to pull herself up now. (*Paula is holding a couple of plums and a banana in her hand, about to put them in the fruit bowl. She stops and looks down at them almost dreamily*)

Bella goes into the kitchen with some shopping

Bella (*off*) The price of bloomin' things nowadays you can hardly afford to live. Forty-nine p they charged me for a small tin of Dutch 'am. That's ten bob in real money. And how much were them bananas?

Paula doesn't answer

Bella comes out of the kitchen. She sees what Paula is doing, comes over and takes them out of her hand and puts them in the fruit bowl

Pack it in, you'll go blind.

Paula Oh I were miles away then Nanna.

Bella I know exactly where you were and it weren't miles away.

Paula Three months—it's been a long time.

Bella Three months—it's been thirty-odd years with me. It's just a memory now love, it's got cobwebs on it.

They carry on putting things away

Paula Nanna, what were me grandad like?

Bella (*stopping what she's doing*) Yer grandad? Oh he wasn't a bad sort really. Lookin' back on it he wasn't any worse than the rest. He drank a lot, but in them days they all did. It were their only escape. Quickest road out of Oldham they called it—the ale-'ouse door. He were a collier when we first met, he come from Barnsley way originally. And I'll never forget on our weddin' night we got into bed—well we'd undressed in the dark, very prim it was in them days, nighties laced up to here—(*she indicates her throat*)—and fastened down to your wrists—any road up the next mornin' the sun was shinin through the window and I looked at his body and it was all smooth and pale. He had a lovely skin. Then I looked at his back and there were tiny blue lines all over it, like veins. Scars they were, that had healed over with the coal dust inside and down his spine on every bone were a scab where he'd banged himself crawling under the pit-props, miners' buttons he used to call them. No wonder he drank so much. He had a hard life in them days. You talk about the good old days, there weren't none. You've got a chance you young 'uns today. You've got time for each other. We were always working or raising kids, or fighting bloody wars. Oh, there were happy days too, and we always kept smiling, always had a laugh. We enjoyed ourselves in our own way, but it was always in spite of, not because of.

Paula Who?

Bella Them, the ones that ran it all, and owned it all and didn't give a bugger about the ordinary people.

Paula goes over to her and puts her arms round her

Paula But you never gave up fighting did you Nan?

Bella Me! The buggers will have to shoot me first.

Paula laughs and kisses her

> *There are noises off and Eileen and Norma come in with more shopping bags, perhaps bulkier things like a couple of pillows*

Eileen Ooh, I've got this funny pain in me chest. I feel all dizzy. I hope it's not me 'eart.

Norma (*ignoring her, to Paula*) Did you get everything love?

Paula Yes, apart from the onions, they looked a bit manky, I've got some that I'll bring round later.

Bella I'll put the kettle on.

> *Bella exits to the kitchen*

Eileen and Norma flop down on the settee

Norma Ee, just the job. Me feet are killing me. (*To Paula*) Have you heard the latest from your dad this mornin' Paula? He had his uniform on and he said—(*she imitates him*)—"I'm going to put a new transmission in a landrover so that when the time comes I can defend you and your Marxist friends in spite of themselves, and stop the Russians sending you all to Siberia."

They laugh

> I said the only Marx I know is the one on the corner of Johnson Street that I get me knickers from.

Bella comes in with the tea

Eileen Well I don't know, it's getting me down a bit now this. I mean it's been three months. I never thought we'd last out. I never was very physical, you know, didn't even like Postman's Knock when I was a kid or going on the hobby-horse in the playground, but I think I'm starting to feel a bit frustrated now. You know this morning I was reaching for something on the top shelf in the kitchen and as I was leaning up against the washing-machine it started going to spin dry and all the vibrations went through me and it got me—— (*she stops*).

Norma What? It got you what? Go on.

Eileen (*beat*) Well, you know.

Norma I don't.

Eileen Yes you do.

Norma No I don't.

Eileen Of course you do.

Norma I bloody well don't.

Bella She does but she wants to hear you tell 'er.

Paula What happened Auntie Eileen?

Eileen Well I don't know how to say really. I mean, I thought, ooh that's nice and I just sort of stayed there and kept it on fast hot wash and spin.

Norma Well, go on.

Eileen Well, then there was a knock at the door and I knew it was the Co-op dairy for his money, and well me legs were all shakin' and that and you know I told you about him, him with the red 'air and the moustache, the really 'andsome one that looks like Jess Conrad, you know the one that keeps smiling at me—he's just got divorced you know by the way. Well, I went to the door and I felt like I was in a dream, I was all twitchy and, and well, hot and shaky and I opened the door and, ooh I feel stupid.

Norma Go on will you, you dozy bugger.

Eileen Well, it was the other one, his little bandy mate with the squint and no teeth, so I just burst out crying and said "No yoghurt on Saturday" and ran back in.

Bella Where does he live, this one with no teeth?

Norma Mother!

Bella Well, I've got that set of Mrs Wetherby's Arnold's. He could have them. I bet I could straighten his eyes for him an' all.

Norma Is that all that happened?

Eileen No, I forgot to cancel the kippers for Sunday, and with all that spinning I shrunk his best shirt.

Norma (*dreamily*) It were funny last night. Nobby got undressed, I was in bed reading and he got undressed and the moonlight was just coming through a crack in the curtains, and he stood by the bed naked and bathed in a sort of golden light and it made his body look all creamy and smooth and young again. You couldn't see his beer belly in the shadows. And I just stared at him all bathed in this golden glow, like a picture he was and I could feel meself sort of aching inside——

They're all listening intently

—then he burped, farted and fell into bed smelling of Guinness and king-prawn vindaloo. So I switched the light on and carried on with me book.

Bella steps to the stage front as the Lights fade slightly

Norma and Eileen exit, taking the shopping bags and mugs with them

Bella Course none of this were affecting me as much as it was the others. Like I say, in my case, it was all like a faded memory. But I felt most sorry of all for Paula.

Paula picks up the baby and rocks her in her arms

I mean she'd only been married a bit, and the point was Ken's heart wasn't really in the army at all. He was sticking it out now because his dad and Nobby had put their feet down, but he only joined the army in the first place 'cos it ran in the family, like squinting or lunacy.

Bella exits

SCENE 3

The same. Late afternoon

Paula is rocking the baby, singing to it softly the old Irish song "The Spinning Wheel"

Ken comes in quietly, watches her for a while

Paula sees him

Paula Oh hello.
Ken Hello, everyone out?
Paula Yes, they're all at church hall putting up our exhibition.
Ken Has she been all right then?
Paula Yes, she's been really good bless her. Her cheeks are all red, I think she's starting with her teeth.

Ken comes and looks over her shoulder. There is a tender moment between them. They are standing behind the settee so there is not much room. She bends slightly to put the baby back in and he finds himself hard up against her. She stands and turns and he turns with her until she is facing the audience and he is standing behind her. They freeze

  Ken! Give up will you.
Ken Oh Paula.
Paula Ken, pack it in!
Ken Oh God.
Paula Oh God, give up Ken will you.
Ken Oh God.
Paula Oh God, stop saying "Oh God".
Ken Oh God I can't.
Paula Ken, it's no good Ken (*clenching her fists*), I'm not going to give in.
Ken I can't help it, I can't move.
Paula Will you give over Ken.
Ken Oh God.
Paula I've told you to stop saying "Oh God". Give up, pack it in, get your hands off. Ooh. (*She is weakening too*)

But Ken is just about to put his arms round her when she makes a noise that starts like a low growl and ends up with her shaking her head from side to side and breaking free from his grasp

  It's no good, I'm not weakening, I'm not going to give in, pack it in.
Ken (*falling over the settee exhausted*) Oh God, Oh God.

  Paula goes out to the kitchen and comes back in

Paula Ken, come here love.

He goes over to her. She kisses him and whilst they're still joined in a kiss she puts her hand on the top of his trousers near the waistband

Ken Ooh, that's nice.

Sexy giggling

Paula Mmmm.
Ken Oooh.
Paula Mmmm.

Ken Oooh.

Paula Mmmm.

Ken (*leaping about*) Ah, you, ah, oh, chuffin' 'eck. Bloody 'ell fire. (*Leaping about and jumping he suddenly stops and opens his fly shaking ice cubes out all over the floor. There are a lot of them*) Bloody ice cubes! You dozy mare!!

Paula You know what you look like Ken? You look just like an eskimo having a pee.

Ken (*shivering*) You dozy bugger (*looking down inside his trousers*), it's like a blue acorn.

Paula Well you know what to do our Kenneth if you ever want the little blue acorn to grow into a big oak tree again, leave the bloody army! Come on anyway, we'd best get home, I've got your tea to make and you can keep your hands to yourself.

Ken scoops up the ice cubes and puts them in the flower vase. He and Paula exit, taking the baby and pram with them.

SCENE 4

The same. Evening

Norma comes in with an ironing-board, some ironing and an iron which she sets up in front of the settee, sideways on to the audience. She starts ironing

Nobby comes in with a newspaper and sits in the armchair reading

Norma Bloomin' 'eck it's nearly ten o'clock, I'll miss the news.

She picks up the radio from the sideboard, takes it near the ironing-board and plugs it in. As soon as she plugs it in the stage goes to darkness, not pitch black but a faint light from perhaps the street outside illuminates just enough for us to see what's happening. Perhaps Nobby could have a cigarette too, that moves with him through the dark as he goes

Nobby (*putting down his newspaper*) What've you done now?

Norma It must be fused or something.

Nobby 'Ave you got a match?

Norma There's one in the sideboard drawer. (*Noises of fumblings in the dark*) Ooh piggin' 'eck I've banged me soddin' shin.

Nobby Don't move I'm coming across.

Norma (*as they bump into each other in the dark*) Oh my God—you frightened me to death then.

Nobby Well who the hell did you think it was? There's only the two of us in the room.

Norma You just frightened me that's all. Ay, pack that in.

Nobby Ooh that's nice.

Norma Let go, Nobby, pack it in will you.

Nobby Ooh.

Norma Pack it in. I've told you, stop it, give up with your nonsense, pack it in, get your 'ands away, gerroff, just keep your hands to yourself.
Nobby Go on love, go on.
Norma Nobby, I can't. It's important this. I'm not foolin' about. None of us is going to give in.
Nobby Oh come on. Come on just give us a cuddle.
Norma I've told you Nobby, don't, pack it in, give up. Give over, what yer—will you stop it. (*Weakening a bit*) Oh don't Nobby, don't, nay—now Nobby now, Nobby, Nobby—Nob-Nobby—(*She's weakening considerably now*) Now Nobby I'm going to get mad in a minute, now. (*Obviously not particularly in control of herself*) Now, ay give up, just give up Nobby. (*Her speech gets quieter and less resistant*) Nobby. Ay now, now give, don't love, now just don't, no don't do, oh, oh.
Nobby Ooh, ow, ah ah. (*Screaming out loud*) Ah, chuffin' 'eck, oh, bloody, piggin' oh, chuffin' 'eck.
Norma What 'ave you done? What 'ave you done?

Nobby jumps about as she finds a match and strikes it

Nobby That chuffin' iron. I've put my chuffin' 'and right on it. Bloody 'ell fire. Chuffin' 'eck.
Norma Come on, I'll put some soap on it.
Nobby It's burnt not dirty, you dozy bugger.
Norma Don't be stupid, it'll stop it stingin'.

They go towards the kitchen. She leads him with a match. We hear Nobby grumbling in pain

You're a big soft kid, it's only a little burn, it's nothing. I thought you were supposed to be a soldier. You're like a big girl's blouse.
Nobby (*as they reach the kitchen*) Well it bloody well 'urts.
Norma (*as they go in*) You're a mardarse, that's what you are.

Nobby and Norma exit to the kitchen

SCENE 5

The same. Morning

As the Lights change, Bella comes in and stands stage front

Bella Well, it were obvious after a bit that this couldn't go on forever, but no-one would give in.

Norma enters with a basket of ironing

We wouldn't, the men wouldn't and it got worse when Nobby and Norma stopped talking to each other entirely. Like two big soft kids.
Norma We'll be starting off at twelve next Saturday, the Rochdale group will be leaving at the same time. They're coming from all over. They reckon about three thousand will be there at the Town Hall.

Bella I just hope the weather stays fine that's all.

Norma (*listening*) He's up, just wait till he comes down here and asks for his shirt.

Bella Ay, and finds out you haven't pressed his uniform trousers either.

Nobby enters in vest and underpants and goes to get his trousers. They are not on the maiden. He sees them in the basket. He pulls them out and they're crumpled up like a concertina. He looks at Norma, opens his mouth as though to say something, then closes it

It's a pity you never learnt to play the concertina our Nobby, you could have got a good tune out of them.

Nobby Ask 'er where me shirt is.

Norma Tell him as far as his shirt's concerned I haven't washed it.

Bella Well I'm not standing here listening to you soft buggers, I'm going down the Evergreen Club to talk to some sensible people. I'll see you later Norma.

Norma Ay, ta-rah Mother.

Bella exits

When Bella has gone there is no intermediary. Nobby stands perplexed for a minute looking at his trousers. Norma stands the iron up and sits down reading the papers. Nobby looks at the iron and goes over. He looks at his bandaged hand ruefully, remembering what happened the last time. He picks it up, reads the setting on it and starts ironing while looking at it closely. He lifts it off, obviously nothing is happening. He presses the steam button and burns himself on the front of his jockey shorts. He hops about for a bit, trying not to shout then he shouts out loud

Nobby Chuffin' piggin' bleedin' 'eck. (*He picks up the iron as though he is about to throw it, changes his mind and puts his trousers on as they are. He finds an old shirt in the washing basket and puts it on, stains and all*)

At that moment the bell rings. Neither of them speak although both of them open their mouths as though to do so. The bell goes again, they look at each other, neither of them says anything. The bell rings again. Again both of them look as though they are going to say something

Eventually Nobby goes to the door angrily. It's Tommy. We hear them talking off

(*Off*) Why didn't you just come in?

Tommy (*off*) You never shouted me to.

As they come in we see that Tommy is as dishevelled as Nobby is, with very crumpled trousers on, a crumpled jacket and a dirty shirt

Nobby You look a right scruffy monkey. You've not even had a shave.

Tommy It's Eileen, she forgot to get me razor blades from Tesco's. Hello Norma.

Norma Hello Tommy.

Nobby (*to Tommy*) Ask her if she's going to do me any clean shirts.

Tommy He says are you goin' to do 'im any clean shirts?

Norma Tell 'im he's a lazy fat slob and he's as much use as a one-legged man in a bum-kicking contest and if he wants his shirts washing, or the skid marks scrubbing off his Y-fronts he can do them himself.

Tommy She says you're a lazy fat slob and——

Nobby (*stopping him*) Come on you daft bugger, I heard what she said.

Nobby and Tommy exit to the hall

Norma carries on ironing

Eileen enters

Eileen Hello Norma.

Norma Hello love, did you see Nobby and Tommy on the way out?

Eileen Ay, they looked as though somebody had found them on a bring and buy stall. Where's Bella?

Norma She's gone down the Evergreen Club, she's reading to her old ladies.

Eileen What does she read to them?

Norma Well, they're supposed to be romances, but they all like westerns or thrillers. She says sometimes she can't sleep at night with the things they make her read. She should be back in a bit. I'm expecting Paula round too. It's baby clinic day. She said Ken went to Bury the other day, chance of a job. There were eight hundred and fourteen blokes queueing up for one job. It had gone by the time he'd got there. (*Noticing for the first time that Eileen is quiet*) You're quiet today—are you all right?

Eileen No not really, I've got something to say and I'd better get it off me chest. I just can't carry it on, me nerves won't take it anymore. (*She snivels a bit*)

Norma (*suspiciously*) What are you talking about? Your nerves won't take it anymore, what do you mean?

Eileen (*snivelling*) I can't be involved any more, in the peace movement, it's makin' me ill. I've got migraines all the time now. I feel like me head's trapped in a vice and my chest's all tight.

Norma (*now strong and determined*) But you can't give in now. We've got them. We've got them worried. We're beatin' them. They'll give in, we've just got to hang on longer, that's all, we've just got to show that we're strong and not give in.

Eileen I can't do it, not any more. (*Seriously and totally convincingly*) I'm not a fighter Norma, you weren't either, but you are now. You've changed. But I'm just not that sort of person.

Norma But you can't give it all up now, Eileen, we've gone too far.

Eileen (*standing*) But I just can't take it Norma, I just can't carry on with it. It's ruining our marriage.

Norma Eileen, if you give this up now, we're all finished.

Eileen (*leaving slowly*) I'm sorry, I just can't do it. I'm going. I'm sorry I've let you down but I'm just not strong enough. It's really upsetting me. I'll see you later.

Eileen exits

Norma (*slamming the iron down*) Shit! (*Quietly, then louder*) Shit! Shit! Shit! They've won. The chuffin' swines have won. (*She sits down deflated and defeated with her head on her arms on the ironing-board*)

After a pause, Paula comes in wheeling the pram

Paula What's up with Auntie Eileen? I just saw her on the other side of the road and waved to her and I don't think she saw me, she just carried on walking.

Norma She's given in—she's leaving us, she says she just can't take it anymore.

Paula I thought there was something funny the other day when she went all quiet. Well, we don't have to give up just because she has.

Norma No, but we've not much chance of winning now.

Paula Ay, I suppose you're right. It will give them all fresh encouragement.

They sit quietly for a minute

Bella comes in wearing her helmet and wellingtons. She starts to take them off

Bella What's up with you two? You've got faces like a wet weekend in a welly works.

Paula Auntie Eileen's left.

Bella Left where?

Paula She's left the peace movement.

Bella I knew she'd do summat to that sort, she always were a spineless mare, well we'll just have to carry on regardless, we're not giving up. I mean there's not just us there's all the other women in the Deepdale Movement.

Norma But we're the only ones that are trying to get our husbands out of the TA.

Bella Well that's true—any road I'll go and put the kettle on, I've got a mouth like a badger's bum.

Bella exits to the kitchen

Paula lifts the baby out of the pram and rocks her gently. There is a low here, a quiet moment.

Bella comes in with the cups and puts them down. She goes to look at the baby

Hello me likkle love, give us a smile, go on give your old granny a smile, that's better. (*To Paula*) What did they say at the clinic?

Paula Everything's fine, she's gaining weight and they said she's contented. They said she's doing great.

Bella Smashin'. Ee, she's a love. You'd wonder how anyone could 'arm 'em wouldn't you?

Bella goes into the kitchen

In another quiet moment, Eileen comes in

Paula (*noticing her*) Hello Auntie Ei.

Bella comes out of the kitchen and stands with the teapot in her hands

Eileen Hello love. (*To Norma, handing her a piece of paper*) Look at this, I've found it in his pocket.

Norma (*scanning the paper, reading it to herself for a while*) Well, the swines—I knew they knew what was going on but they wouldn't let on.

Paula What does it say?

Norma Listen to this. (*She reads*) "Ministry of Defence classified document. To be circulated to all officers, TAVR regiments UK. This document is classified, anyone disclosing parts or all of this document to unqualified personnel shall be deemed to be guilty of an offence under The Defence of the Realm Act, nineteen forty-two. This document supplements Field Order Training Manual TAVR-five-QP-nine-one-seven, nineteen seventy-six, civil defence civil disorder contingency plans UK nuclear war/disaster. In the time of a declared emergency the TAVR units remaining in the UK will form part of five infantry brigade for the purposes of home defence. In this role they will be assigned to the various military commissioners. The military will take precedence over the civil in all matters relating to the emergency. Duties will be the policing of key communication centres (telephone exchanges, television and radio stations etc.), food stores and regional seats of government. The military role will include the rounding-up of disaffected seditious personnel and of suspects. It is expected that subversive elements in the civilian population will try to stir unrest. They will be known to the police from information located on the main computers at Bristol. The role of the military will be to secure internment camps and to put under armed guard subversives, rioters, looters etc. and such people as the Government may deem fit to be interned. Further roles will be the imposition of a curfew on the civilian population and the enforcement of laws under the Special Emergency Powers Act nineteen seventy-three. Under the command of the local military, the territorials will also be expected to patrol the streets quelling any unrest and riot. In such a role they will be expected to perform as the Army has performed in Northern Ireland (using the yellow card system). They may be expected to fire upon civilians found looting, rioting or behaving in any other way in a suspicious manner. The military may also be called upon to perform public executions in the case of local commanders having decreed civilians or military personnel to have been guilty of capital crimes, or to be of grave danger to the community. This could also include the execution of possibly infected personnel from radiated or diseased zones, or personnel trying to enter prohibited zones." Well, that caps it all! My God!

Bella I told you, they damn well know all that were goin' on, they knew it all the time.

Eileen Well, if they think I'm giving in now, they've got another piggin' think comin'. (*Beside herself with anger*) I-I-I could bloody kill our Kenneth.

Norma It says here they're calling the TAVR up for a weekend of counter revolutionary and nuclear, biological and chemical warfare at Fulwood Barracks, Preston. The swines.

Paula We don't just have to take it though, do we Mum?

Norma No, you're right. They may be going on this course, but there's nothing to stop us going up there ourselves.

Eileen What could we do?

Norma We can demonstrate outside the gates.

Paula I think it would be even more effective if we had a vigil. Just us.

Bella You're right love.

Paula If we stand vigil all night, we'll be like, like witnesses.

Eileen Just the four of us.

Paula It'll be more effective.

Norma A silent vigil.

Paula Yes.

Bella Well, as silent as I can keep. If I see our Nobby I won't be able to stop meself from wanting to kick his backside.

They start to ready themselves

Norma Well, couldn't you do it quietly?

Bella Ay, I could muffle me boots so that they don't make such a noise when they meet his bum.

Eileen (*suddenly manic*) If I see our Tommy and our Ken, I'll, I'll bleedin' kill 'em.

The others do a double-take

Black-out

SCENE 6

There is the sound of wind in the trees, occasional traffic and somewhere a bird singing

The Lights come up—early evening. A sign descends from the flies—"MOD TAVR Barracks Supply and Training Depot, Fulwood"

The women come on slowly in overcoats, carrying flasks, bags etc. The baby is in a sling on Paula's chest. She unslings her and holds her in her arms

Bella By 'eck, it's a bit brass-monkey, isn't it. It's a good job I've got me thermals on.

Eileen It's a bit dark in't it. I hope there's no funny fellas about.

Bella Well, it'd keep you warm anyway.

Paula I've got a couple of pair of Ken's football socks on.

She shows them—the atmosphere is warm and humorous. They plant a banner saying "Deepdale Women's Peace Vigil" and settle down. As the light fades they light candles. They sing the Greenham Common Women's song, "You Can't Kill the Spirit." Paula begins singing on her own then the others join in until the song fills out. When they've finished Bella flaps her arms trying to get warm, no easy job while you're holding a candle in one hand

Bella I've got icicles on me tricicles. Do you think they'd mind if we chopped that notice down and made a fire?

Norma You'd get six months for destroying Government property.

Bella Well I wouldn't mind, think of all the money I'd save on food and gas, anyway they reckon there's a better class of criminal in prison nowadays.

Norma (*to an unseen policeman*) Evening, Officer.

Eileen Ay, that's right, another load of woolly minds in woolly hats, that's what we are. (*Under her breath to the others*) He nearly smiled then, humourless pillock.

They sit quietly supporting each other, the candles burning brightly

Woolly minds in woolly hats.

Norma They just can't see, can they?

Paula It's a funny thing, but I think that really you'll never convince some people. They've made their minds up and they'll never change them.

Norma All you can do is stand up and show them you won't be counted in with them.

Bella Ay, if we don't do it, who will?

Dawn slowly rises, birds sing and from off we hear the sound of soldiers' quick-marching. The quick marching gets louder and louder until the audience gets the impression that a troop of soldiers are quick-marching across stage. It should be loud and menacing, but not so loud that the women's voices can't be heard totally clearly over the sound of marching

(*Good-humouredly*) Go on, you should be back with your mammy, son. Ay, don't you stick two fingers up at me. I'd kick your backside for you if I wasn't in the peace movement. You're not too big you know.

Paula On your bike, go on.

Norma Come for your blood money 'ave you?

Eileen (*starting them all off*) One two three four, we don't want to go to war, two four six eight, we don't want to radiate.

They all chant it a couple of times

Bella Don't talk to me like that, sonny. If you had brains you'd be dangerous.

Norma Here's our lot.

Nobby, Tommy and Ken come on, fast-marching, camouflaged and wearing branches in their helmets, carrying their weapons, gas masks etc. As far as possible, they should be made to look comical rather than menacing

Nobby (*shouting loudly*) Left right, left right, left right.

Bella (*loudly*) Our Nobby, come here.

Nobby Mother, what the bloody 'ell. (*He's flummoxed*)

Bella Never mind that, you can get home now, straight away.

Nobby (*like a little boy*) Mother, mother don't talk daft.

Eileen And you our Kenneth.

Ken Mam, what are you talkin' about?

Paula Isn't it time you grew up Ken and stopped playing soldiers. Come on, come home.

Ken What are you lot doing 'ere?

Paula We've been here all night.

Ken What about Lucy in all this cold?

Paula She's warm enough and anyway I want her to be part of all this, it's her life we've been fighting for.

Norma What are you going to do with us Nobby when it all starts?

Nobby What do you mean?

Norma Well you're going to have to lock us up aren't you—or shoot us, because we aren't going to let you take us to war this time, not like they did before. You'll have to drag us kicking and screaming through the gates.

Eileen Here you are, Tommy, you can have this back. (*She gives him the paper*)

Tommy If my CO knows you've seen this I'll be up shit creek in a barbed-wire canoe with no paddle.

Paula Ken come on home.

Nobby (*nastily*) I've just about had enough of you lot. (*Menacing*) Now go on, bugger off home the lot of you. Get out of it. Now!! (*Madder*) Do you hear me? You stupid bitch. Get back home where you bloody well belong.

Norma All right Nobby, I will do, I'll go.

Nobby Good.

Norma No you don't understand Nobby, I mean I'm going—not home, I'm going, I'm leaving you.

Nobby You what? What are you talking about? You can't do!

Norma I can and I will. I should have done it long ago, long before now. You'll never change will you, never learn. You still think it's cowboys and indians, well it isn't any more Nobby. You and your generals and your politicians are stupid enough to destroy this world. I might have been fighting you but at the same time I was fighting all those people behind you, the majors, and the colonels, the generals and the dumb chuffin' politicians.

Nobby Don't talk rubbish.

Norma You'll never understand, will you Nobby? Not as long as you've got a hole in your backside, well I'm going.

Nobby Where are you goin'?

Norma Anywhere, I don't care any more, somewhere else where I can do some good, Greenham Common, anywhere.

Paula I'm coming too Mam.

Ken Paula!

Paula I've got to, Ken, don't you see, this fight's too important to let it die now.

Ken Oooh chuffin' 'eck! (*He throws his rifle down and struggles out of his kit*)

Nobby Where are you goin', soldier?

Ken Home.

Nobby Get back in line, soldier.

Ken No Nobby I can't.

Nobby That's an order.

Ken Stuff your orders. Don't you see. It's impossible. I can't do it. I've got

to make me choice. It's her or (*indicating uniform*) this, I've chosen,
Nobby.

Nobby That's desertion you know.

Ken Well, that's tough, come on Paula.

Nobby (*coming out of his authoritative role*) You're not giving in are you
Ken?

Ken (*tiredly*) No, not really, I'm not giving in Nobby, but I've been thinking
about it for quite a while, a long while. We're trained to fight aren't we
Nobby? We're trained to fight an enemy in the field, man to man, gun to
gun, conventional warfare, professional soldiers. We know what we're
doing. This lot—(*indicating the camp notice*)—isn't anything to do with
that sort of soldiering is it? This is mass murder we're talking about here.
I'm a soldier not a murderer, come on love.

Ken and Paula start to leave with the others

Nobby I'll put you on a charge soldier. I'll put you on a charge!

Ken (*as they go*) You do that Nobby—you do.

 They exit, leaving the stage empty except for Nobby and Tommy

Tommy (*gathering Ken's equipment*) D'you think they mean it, Nobby?

Nobby Chuffin' 'eck!

*The Lights die and we get the impression of false tabs. A spot comes up and
Bella steps forward into the light*

Bella Well, that's the way it could have ended and knowing our Nobby it's
more than likely. But there's another way it could have ended too. I'm not
saying which way it did end or which way it should end. Just that there's
another way it might have ended.

SCENE 7

The Lights come up on the living-room—morning

Norma is packing some things in a case

Nobby comes in. He's in uniform but wearing the minimum

Norma I don't want you watching me go, Nobby.

Nobby I haven't come to watch you go.

Norma What do you mean?

Nobby I've resigned.

Norma You what?

Nobby I've just written it out, I'm jackin' the TA.

Norma What about your pension and that?

Nobby Tough, I'll get some, it won't be much. It won't be as much as I'd get
if I stayed in but I'll get something.

Norma (*quietly*) So what changed your mind?

Nobby It was what Ken said more than anything else. I thought about this
lark for a long time and I still couldn't see it your way. I still can't fully,

not yet. I mean I've been trained to think as a soldier in a lot of ways but a couple of things made me think, and then Ken sort of capped it all, he's right I'm a soldier too, not a murderer. Tommy's left too.

Norma Is this true? Are you serious?

Nobby Never been more serious in me life. (*Going to her and kissing her tenderly*) So that's that then.

Norma Oh Nobby. (*She gives him a cuddle*) But I'm not stopping working for the peace movement.

Nobby I don't expect you to, you never know I might end up giving a hand. So that's that then. (*He starts taking his trousers off*) Come on. It's been a long time.

Norma What are you doin'?

Nobby I'm giving you two minutes' start, come on. (*He hops around, removing more of his clothes*)

Norma (*laughing and starting to undress too*) Two minutes? You'd better not be that long.

Nobby, now down to shirt and underpants, over-balances and puts his hand on the ironing-board to steady himself. He burns his hand on the iron, nearly falling over with lots of swearing

Nobby, you're hopeless. Come on love.

They run off to bed

As they go, Bella comes in, pushing the pram

She looks round and sees all the clothes. As she starts picking them up, the ceiling light starts swinging and the noise of a bed squeaking can be heard. The baby gurgles and snuffles a bit. Bella picks her up and sings to her as she rocks her in her arms, singing the old song "Dance to Your Daddy". The Lights slowly fade, as flakes of plaster float down from above

CURTAIN

FURNITURE AND PROPERTY LIST

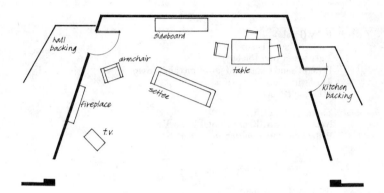

ACT I

SCENE 1

On stage: Settee
Armchair
Chairs
Table. *On it:* tablecloth, party food (sandwiches, cakes, lettuce, dish of
mustard etc.) covered by another tablecloth
Fireplace. *Next to it:* **Bella**'s slippers
TV
Pram. *In it:* nappies, talcum powder etc.
Sideboard. *On it:* bottles of drink including Scotch, beer, Guinness,
various glasses, vase, fruit bowl, radio. *In it:* box of dominoes, notepad
and pen, box of matches
(*Note: some of the props listed above are required for later scenes*)

Off stage: Gun **(Nobby)**
Tray, cake tins containing party food **(Tommy)**
Baby **(Paula)**
Handbag containing paracetamol tablets **(Norma)**
Glass of water **(Nobby)**
Plate of ham **(Norma)**

Personal: **Eileen:** handkerchief

SCENE 2

Off stage: Tray with 3 plates of food and cutlery **(Norma)**
             Pot of tea **(Bella)**
             Pram and baby **(Bella)**

SCENE 3

Off stage: Cup of tea **(Bella)**

SCENE 4

Off stage: Baby **(Paula)**
             Crate of beer **(Tommy)**
             3 glasses of beer **(Nobby)**
             Plate of sandwiches and jar of piccalilli **(Ken)**
             Tray with cups of tea **(Ken)**
             Milk-jug **(Paula)**

Personal: **Eileen:** handkerchief
             Nobby, Tommy, Ken: £1 notes in pockets
             Bella: newspaper cutting in pocket

SCENE 5

Off stage: Baby in sling **(Paula)**
             Knife and lunchbox **(Norma)**
             Jacket **(Nobby)**
             Lunchbox **(Tommy)**
             Plate of food **(Nobby)**
             Baby in sling **(Paula)**

SCENE 6

Off stage: Materials for banner—pins, paints, brushes, banner etc., magazine
             (Norma and **Eileen)**
             Pram **(Paula)**
             Tray with 4 cups of tea **(Paula)**

ACT II

SCENE 1

Strike: Tray with cups of tea
             Banner, paints, pins etc.
             Pram and baby

Off stage: Furry hat **(Ken)**
             3 mugs of tea **(Ken)**

Personal: **Ken:** wrist-watch

SCENE 2

Off stage: Shopping bag containing food items **(Bella)**
           Shopping bag containing food items including plums and a banana; pram
               and baby **(Paula)**
           Shopping bag **(Norma)**
           Shopping bag **(Eileen)**
           Tray with 4 mugs of tea **(Bella)**

SCENE 3

Off stage: Ice cubes **(Paula)**

SCENE 4

Off stage: Ironing-board, iron and clothes **(Norma)**
           Newspaper **(Nobby)**

SCENE 5

Off stage: Basket of clothes including **Nobby**'s crumpled trousers and shirt; maiden
               (Norma)
           Pram and baby **(Paula)**
           3 cups **(Bella)**
           Piece of paper **(Eileen)**
           Teapot **(Bella)**

SCENE 6

Set: Camp sign

Off stage: Bags, banner, flasks, candles, matches **(Norma, Bella, Eileen)**
           Baby in sling **(Paula)**
           Gas masks, weapons **(Nobby, Ken, Tommy)**

Personal: **Eileen:** paper in pocket

SCENE 7

Strike: Camp sign, bags, flasks etc.
           Pram

Set: Case and clothes for **Norma**

Off stage: Pram and baby **(Bella)**

LIGHTING PLOT

Property fittings required: pendant light, fire effect, TV effect
Apart from one exterior, all the scenes are interior—a living-room

ACT I

To open: Full general lighting

ACT II

To open: General interior lighting—evening—pendant and fire effect on

Cue 16 **Nobby** exits to kitchen with mugs   (Page 31)
        Change lighting to mid-afternoon

Cue 17 **Norma:** "... with me book."   (Page 34)
        Fade lights slightly

Cue 18 **Bella** exits   (Page 34)
        Increase lighting slightly—late afternoon

Cue 19 **Ken** and **Paula** exit with pram   (Page 36)
        Change to evening lighting—pendant and fire effect on

Cue 20 **Norma** plugs in radio   (Page 36)
        Black-out, apart from fire effect

Cue 21 **Nobby** and **Norma** exit to kitchen   (Page 37)
        Bring up general interior lighting—morning

Cue 22 **Eileen:** "... bleedin' kill 'em."   (Page 42)
        Black-out

Cue 23 When ready   (Page 42)
        Bring up general exterior lighting—early evening

Cue 24 Women settle down   (Page 42)
        Begin slow fade to darkness

Cue 25 **Bella:** "... who will?"   (Page 43)
        Gradually bring up dawn lighting

Cue 26 **Nobby:** "Chuffin' 'eck!"   (Page 45)
        Black-out; pause, then bring up spot on **Bella**

Cue 27 **Bella;** "... might have ended."   (Page 45)
        Bring up general interior lighting—morning

Cue 28 **Bella** sings to the baby   (Page 46)
        Slowly fade to Black-out

EFFECTS PLOT

ACT I

MADE AND PRINTED IN GREAT BRITAIN BY
LATIMER TREND & COMPANY LTD PLYMOUTH

MADE IN ENGLAND